MW00831723

Lattice of the Years

by
Alice Major

*To Professor Zitnel,
with thanks

Alice Major*

Poems   *Bayeux*

Lattice of the Years
Alice Major
© Copyright 1998 by Bayeux Arts

Published by:
Bayeux Arts Incorporated
119 Stratton Crescent S.W.
Calgary, Alberta, Canada T3H 1T7

P.O. Box 586
1, Holway Point,
Machias, Maine 04654, USA

Spantech House
Lagham Road, South Godstone
Surrey RH9 8HB, UK

Design: Brian Dyson, Syntax Media Services
Cover photograph: Ashis Gupta

Printed and bound in Canada

The publisher gratefully acknowledges
the assistance of the Alberta Foundation
for the Arts and the Canada Council.

Canadian Cataloguing in Publication Data

Major, Alice
  Lattice of the years

  Poems.
  ISBN: 1-896209-25-4

  I. Title.
PS8576.A515L37 1998   C811'.54   C98-911035-4
PR9199.3.M3454L37 1998

For David

Poems from this manuscript have been published in:
Arc
Antigonish Review
The Fiddlehead
Other Voices
People's Poetry Newsletter
Poetry Canada Review
Prairie Journal
Prism international
Queen's Quarterly
Room of Ones Own
Vintage 95 (League of Poets competition anthology)
Whetstone

and broadcast on:
Alberta Anthology (CBC radio)
Writing on the Wall (Women's Television Network)

Contents

I. Symmetry Group

In mathematics, "symmetry" refers to various kinds of transformation that leave something apparently unchanged. Examples are rotation around a centre of symmetry or reflection in an axis. Some other symmetries are:

"Translation symmetry," defined as "rigid motion in the plane" — in other words, shifting a shape to another location without changing its dimensions.

"Glide symmetry," which involves two motions — reflection in an axis plus a translation (a shift in space).

"Dilation symmetry," which results from increasing all dimensions in the same proportion so that the overall shape stays the same.

1. Symmetries of the plane

Was it a happy childhood?

What's the answer, except
we never see the pattern
in absolute symmetry.
Indistinguishable, it looks
the same in all directions.

Five-year diary. A book of tiny pages,
each page mapped in still-smaller tiles,
five lines a day. One day reflected
in the next. The lattice of the years
repeating.
　　　　　A trellis-work of summers—
"We went swimming at the Lions Pool."
Bright chlorine afternoons, the splash
and aqua glitter, the blue-limned grid
that wavered underneath the squealing surface.
Balancing to keep my shoes and underpants
clear of the lukewarm water　puddled
on the change-room floor. Was it that
summer, or the next, when I baby-sat
the next-door neighbour's rabbit? Learned
to draw a filigree of interlacing circles
with compass and coloured pencils.
Lime green and cerise.

Going back to school and back to school
in a new skirt or with a new
vinyl-and-tapestry purse big enough
to hide my hopes in, just like all
the other girls. The crushes
on indistinguishably fair-haired boys,

the days by myself at the bluffs above
Lake Ontario's blue ache. "I wish
I had a friend."

The catalogues of birthday gifts:
hair-brush sets, film for my camera,
shells for my aquarium, and always
"a box of chocolates from Daddy."
And Daddy always getting drunk at Christmas
when presents cost a lot and there was
never any work.   Tension baked
into the sugar cookies, iced over with
pink and green.

Was it that year or the next when
I lost my school books and was
terrified of telling — they'd cost
so much. Was it that year
or the next when I wrote "I wish
something, something about
making Mummy happy."

> *Love and pain. How to collapse*
> *the pattern? Find*
> *an axis labelled "happy" or*
> *"unhappy"? It was just one*
> *wide plane. Put the mirror down*
> *anywhere, see*
> *the same thing.*

II. Symmetries of translation

The murmur of the television news from down the hall.
My parents' voices quiet, their end-of-day words
blurred, as though they spoke some language
I could almost understand. I lay cramped
by the pressure of stuffed toys. I didn't have the heart
to put them on the floor — their feelings might be hurt.

                    And I thought about
love, feeling for it like a pillow in the dark room.
Love was so important to the little women
of my books.

Don't I love Mummy and Daddy?
I reached into the darkness for some
shape that I could understand and cling to,
panic rising at the dead air in my chest.
Don't I love anyone?

     Shift
     twelve years, one suburb away.
     The young husband in the bed beside me.
     I say to him, "I love you, I love
     you," too often — mantra and apology and
     filler, like the chopped onions and celery
     I pile into our macaroni dinners to
     stretch and disguise them. "I love you too," he
     answers by rote.
     These seem to be the only words we know
     in a foreign tongue. Barely enough
     to negotiate the basic transactions.
               The bed still seems too crowded. I strain
               as if to hear words spoken down the hall,
               speech I have not learned to translate.

III. Bilateral symmetry

Dance floor   someone's wedding
and the deejay spinning a slow, remembered tune
— music coiling off the cassette
like double-sided tape   peeled from its backing

we press
front to front
fingertip to fingertip
our hands
coupled
left for right
right for left
limb for limb we mirror
match

I glance up — your mouth
is tucked around a half-smile
we are equally
amused
by our languorous
twin   lust

but the heart is an asymmetric system —
blood flows in one
direction only   forced
by the squeeze of muscle through
the forked arteries   caught
and held again in the heart's
right chamber

I love you
I murmur in your ear
to keep the beat

IV. Glide symmetry

Music hovers, a long tender wing
in this nursery-sized room.
Outside the door, the ward is quiet
for once. It is Yom Kippur, a day
choked with memories. Gliding
from the tape recorder — Kol Nidre,
the yearning voice of Israel.
      Your mother is gazing out the window
      where September sky floats, cantorial,
      clear away. Streaks of high cirrus
      pencil the blue, curved gently at the ends
      like the curls of a good child.
And you watch her. Her pink sweater
buttoned high across her chest.
            Your eyes are dark and bright
            together, a reflection of tears.
The years have slipped aside, like beads
    displaced along a string. Child reflects
parent. Now it is your hand that folds her
      fingers around a plastic cup of milk
          to help her drink.
          The music ends. Into the silence
          your mother says, "He has a cry
          in his voice." As if the words
      had floated to her from a years-ago
September. Her lucid moment hovers.
          We reach for it — a swan's
          white feather drifting down.

V. Symmetries of dilation

Early griefs lay down the shape —
as a baby nautilus creates
    with its first seed-chamber
    the opalescent model
        for its unfolding
        growth.

Death of a pet turtle. Its small life taken
for granted. But, in the ritual —
    the pastel roses cut from birthday cards
    and pasted on a cardboard box, the hollow
        dug with a spoon from the kitchen drawer —
        sadness swallows us.
We feel again the scrabble of minute claws
against our palm, remember the sideways
    scoop of stubby legs. In wrapping
the shallow-domed shell with pink tissue,
        we come to know completely
        that the narrow head will never
emerge again. Remember our delight?
that first time, when we saw the cords
    stretch beneath the pleated skin
    and the miniature jaws
        open.
The newer griefs grow larger, but
no different in shape. The great griefs
loom ahead. Their mouths open wider
    and wider, create
    the laminate structure of loss —
    sea creatures building a universe
        of spiralled pearl. Hold that opening
        to your ear and listen
        to the empty
            palaces

II. These are not my bones

These are not my bones

D'you think her toes are turning in?
Your anxious voice above my head
in the High Street's 'better' shoe store.

Me looking through the peephole
of the x-ray machine, a 1950s periscope
made to peer through leather. Green glow.
My toe-bones wiggle like fossils come to life,
shadows moving on an ocean floor. Not my bones
surely. They must belong to someone else.

Don't scliff your feet like that.
Walk over the Leven bridge, its steep back
humped over a Scottish stream.

Me too small to see the other side —
crouched to peer between stone pillars
as the water swirls below.

You in your cloth coat, trim ankles; baby sister
tucked in the pram like a winkle. We're off
to West-bridge-end to visit aunts, have tea
and purchase kippers in MissisGillis' shop.
I'll get a bag of dolly mixture if I'm good,
pick up my feet.

You walk just like your mother!
Sister-in-law behind me sounds
surprised. But I already know
that I climb stairs like you — one
hand on my knee at the top step.

Now I have climbed the hump
of the bridge, can see the far half
of my life. And I know that these are not
my bones. I wear my flesh over an old
identify of heel, tarsus, shin —
shell memories in an ancient sea.

I walk with you
in me.

Family picnic up Loch Lomond-side

. . . in a country and a time where sandwiches were always
cut in quarters, not in greedy halves. The carful of cousins
like a wriggle of fish in a net. One uncle had the car,
another owned the television set — technology spread thin
throughout the clan like margarine on white bread.

The impatience of bathing suits bunched
beneath our clothes. Mine a rucked material
pressing concertina edges in my skin.

The islands — Inchmurrin, Inchcailloch — moored solemnly
off the narrow dock of beach. Cloud flotillas cast shadows,
warship-grey. Fires were lit to comfort kettles.

In the frolic meant to conquer goosebumps, stones and breeze,
I capsized into deeper water. I kept my eyes open,
as my father taught me to, diving for ha'pennies
in the safe transparent water of the public baths

— and saw looming from the shadowed cold a shape
to trouble dreams. Flattened limbs like flippers
of a giant turtle, a stretching neck, a darker green
under green. I scrambled wild arms and legs for surface.

On the beach again, I sat on scratchy gravel, ate
egg sandwich between hiccups, drank sweet tea
from thermos lids.

It was a log. Just your imagination. Reassurances
like the thin towel on my shoulders. The cloud ships steamed
along the loch, left sun to leap about on wavelets.
I watched the sparkle, thought about the strange things
underneath, shivered at the flimsy barrier between
me and monsters.

Wool villanelle

My arms are tired from holding out the skein
while Nana winds the yarn into a ball.
Soft wool a halter lying on my skin.

First her fingers bend a loop, and then
a tiny fetus. She binds its limbs, methodical.
My arms are tired holding out the skein.

The ball grows plump and smooth, bumps tamed.
"Hold up your hands," she says, imperial.
Wool a soft halter lying on my skin.

Back and forth the rhythm, a refrain
of structured motion. Dip and rise and fall.
My arms are weary holding out the skein.

"Hold up your hands," Nana says again.
Chatelaine and Fate, her rule inexorable.
Soft wool a halter lying on my skin.

The last few fetters loosen their lacy chain.
The end falls off my arm. She tucks it in the ball.
My arms drop, tired from holding out the skein.
Soft wool a halter lying on my skin.

Saying again

"Say that again." Circle of faces
in the itchy schoolyard.

Hot-faced in my woolen kilt and jumper —
no, sweater. I had to learn its name
all over.

You didn't need jumpers
not in May, in this country
where the sun was so hot
where the sun was so bright
and the streets so wide and
empty, green front lawns
vast as prairie.

Say that again. I soon learned
not to say it. Not to pull the sound
of "book" into "boo-ik." Or "good"
into "guid."
Clip it off short. Learn to wear shorts
in the hot season.

Say it again.
Good.

Sea Horse

What is a country, after all,
but the shadow of some mythic beast
projected on the roundness
of a sphere — the two-dimensional
skin of a tale told often.

Upon a time, when my days spun long
and legendary, bedtime was an arbitrary mark
on the clock's train-ticketing face. My bed
lay flat and quiet as a station platform
after the engine leaves. In the twilight
I curled on my side, stared up at my wall,
at the map of the world.
                        Found my
country. Imagined it a pink horse rearing
from the sea — Hudson's Bay like a saddle
on its back, rising to the high pommel
of Ungava. Its tail lashed the ocean
with arabesque peninsulas — Avalon,
Cape Race, Cape Sable. Names flung
like fine spray on my face.

What did I feel for it? For this
name I sang in the pink-tongued
morning classroom? OHHH CANaDAH.
The tune boring. The words orotund
as small planets in our mouths.

My map-shadow was big. I liked that.
As though we'd won some competition.
And even though I lived so small
in it. A few streets, a schoolyard,
a ravine with squirrel voices,
sumac leaves.

How could I know   its size
was part illusion, a trick
of flattening, a fiction shaped
by the spreading of a sphere.

Still, it was big. I learned a true tale
of its distance, told in the chuff of train wheels
all the way to Winnipeg. I was baggage, travelling
with my Scottish grandmother. She couldn't
comprehend a trip of thirty-seven hours and cried
all night, so sure we'd missed our stop.

But, for me, legends wakened with the dawn
in mist whispered from lakes. Sumac scrawled
red crayon fingers at the foot of granite cliffs.
Rock rose from water, pink and fabulous
as my sea horse in the new light of the sun.

What is a country after all
but a tale of lakes and leaves,
a myth of schoolrooms,
a certain size and shape
cast on the curvature
of thought.

Looking for Narnia

All those ardent hours, waiting for surfaces
to dissolve — ten years old and scrunched
in a clothes cupboard. Smell of dust and hopeful
cardboard, the sharp bite of shoe heels
against my shins, the sensible sensation of cloth
coats hung against my face. I was waiting
for the scuffed paint to release its hold,
let me through to that deep reality,
to the scent of pines and snow that must
inform my humdrum world with the rumour
of talking beasts.

Always brought up
short against all the
incorrigible surfaces
that hemmed me in.

I longed in front of mirrors in the twilight,
sure that spells could bring the numinous
to touch my face, sure I could see
the lady in green silk who offers heart's
desire, sure that fernseed — could I only
find it to lay on my eyelids — would let light
through from the other countries
where beasts embrace speech.

Light always re
flected back. I
could never
get behind wall or
mirror's stubborn
silver to that real
world.

Queen Anne's Lace

You knew the decorative value
of words.
    "Mary,"
you said to the young wife
wiping porridge from the baby's tray,
in the basement suite where beige
neutralized the space,
    "There's a gallon of white left
    from that last job. I could dirty it down
    with some burnt umber — just to make it cover —
    and paint the living room for you."

    "Dirty white?" she
wrinkled her nose. "I don't think
I'd like that."

So you communed with the pastel poetry
of paint chips lined up on battered cards
in the locker across the hall.

    "Mary," you said this time,
while the potatoes were boiling
and steam was patterning the small, high windows
that looked out onto car wheels,
    "How would you like the living room painted in

    Queen Anne's Lace."

The very name a gift.

    "Yes, that sounds pretty."
And next Sunday you went to the locker,
stirred a little burnt umber into
the gallon of white.

"Hold on tight,"
you ordered the children when we took turns
to help you shake the canvas drop sheets
after you finished a job. Our small arms stretched
like pages poised behind a nobleman
in all his robes.
                    And when we held on tight
enough and dropped the corners fast
enough, the snap
sneezed dust
and flecks of paint into the air.

      Empire
         gold.
      Wedgewood
        blue.
      Queen
         Anne's
            Lace.

A cloud of coloured words, weaving finery—
paint chips catching like a coronet
in our hair.

Lighthouse keeper

The shortest distances are hardest
to cross. What can a mother do? Flash warnings
like a blinkered lighthouse trapped
on a coast where the dangers are known
too well.

       "Lots of fish in the sea," you told her.
You wanted her to make far voyage, reach
lands of spice and mine, spin over seas
so remote and bounteous that waves would
toss foam and flying fish at her feet.

Not without peril. That you did not expect.
There would be the dreadful ocean, the whirl
of storm birds, the pinnace cresting towers
of water like a gull's heart breasting air.
                    And perhaps not
ever to come back — you thought of that too, breath
closed in your throat like a jewel snapped shut
in a box when you recognize how dear it is.

But, you told yourself, she likely would
come back, radiant and piratical, tales
landing in a spray at your feet.

You didn't think of this, of her beating before
a wind so close to shore and the old, grey sea —
flinging herself at dangers so terribly
familiar. And you cannot reach her. The wind
drives words back into your mouth
before you utter them.

Slow air

She is packing up her life   and the terrible power
of the tangible takes hold of her in its fist.
No time of life to move again, she thinks. No time
to squeeze your life in yet another, smaller space.

> and remembers that first uprooting,
> holding tight to her daughter's hand as the tender
> steamed over grey water, away from Greenock pier —
> listening to the piper and the skirling gulls
> lament and call her back.

That first chest unpacked in Canada — so little still remains.
It held mostly children's toys. The doll's dress cut
from her wedding gown. Two brass candlesticks;
some wee bit china. A kettle, brought to sing
the small songs of home, of staying put.

> Oh, these men, these men, these wanderers
> who insist "We can't stay here."
> Like the many generations who left
> the moors and crofts empty   to the slow air
> moving over the heartsore hills.

And now, again, so little that can go with her — so much
that reaches out and calls to her, "stay, oh stay."
No room. No room. And everything a memory.
No room for the kitchen table where they would sit
and laugh and fight and cry and sing "westering home."
No room in her chest for breath, her heart squeezed tight.

Living through the war

My father polishes his stories
of survival in a seniors' co-op —
Albert, the inflamed socialist.
Thelma, in the print wrapper,
who waddles down to coffee hour
and snaffles all the chocolate biscuits.
The lost keys and *esprit de corps*.
The daily damage reports — the blitz
of hurt feelings and broken hips.
"It's like living through the war,"
he says. "You keep wondering
who'll go next."

And we're off on stories of the war,
the funny ones that made us think
"the war" had been a comedy routine,
slapstick, Laurel and Hardy in the navy.
Dad a wild teenager in a Cairo police station
hunkered behind an upturned table
spraying all comers with the fire extinguisher.
The court-martial that kept him behind
while his tanker sailed on.

If there was an enemy in the war,
it was a gray and faceless background
to bright-lit cameraderie, to high jinks
and hey-day intensity.

Later, in Chapham Barracks, he met
a friend, the sole survivor
when the tanker slid flaming
into the black Mediterranean.

"An awful nice guy. He had a breakdown.
He just wanted to get out, get back
to his family..."

My father's voice is suddenly
full of tears. Something new has slipped
through the net of old anecdote.
"I just meant to tell a funny story,"
he says with a child's hiccup,
his eyes intensely bright against
the gray and faceless shadow
at his shoulder.

Ember days

He wants to believe in something
that goes on, some echo of beliefs
that chimed so clearly
when he was a wee boy
tough and bright as gorse.

The days shorten
from equinox to solstice
and the feast days turn like
the wheels of a lumbering old cart.

Martinmas, when servants go
to new masters and cattle
are slaughtered.

Feast of Saint Clements,
oranges and lemons gleam
out of the shortening days.

All Souls, when ghosts
flicker on the hillside

Farmers gave him frostbitten turnips
for the peddler's horse. Hunchbacked
Wullie Lang, no taller than the wee boy
who sat beside him as they poked
away up the loch road, pots and pans
clinking and the slosh of kerosene.

Reliquaries and bone fires.
Days of small things. Ringing day
when church bells repeal
the gunpowder plot.
Saint Catherine's Day
and fireworks whizzing round.

So short a time ago. Now he sits
with an old friend who is dying
in a ward where the paint fades to gray.
"I'd like to come back as a seagull,"
he says. "Just wheeling up there."

"Have you ever seen a seagull up close?"
replies his friend. "They have mad eyes."

> *Dismal days - dies mali, the days*
> *of bad luck. Crossed fingers*
> *against the click of beetle*
> *in quiet houses and the death watch.*

So short a time it's been since
the heavy wheels creaked
up the loch shore, past Luss,
as far as Crianlarich
under the ghost-brooding hills.

> *Then, glowing at the centre of the year,*
> *comes Ember Week, Saint Lucy's Day*
> *of lighted candles.*
> *And what comes after that?*

And what comes after that.
He wants to think it all begins again,
and better — better than ever,

that we spiral up and up
like laverocks lifting out of heather,
like gulls in the circle of wind.

Hands speak of mourning

Inarticulate embroidery. The silence
of hands. This is not fine work, simply
a tea cozy in coarse linen.
Simple stitches — the nubble of French knots,
the slip of raised satin stitch.
Simple colours — pink and teacup blue,
leaf green.

It could come from anywhere. Any
great-aunt's drawer or seniors' jumble sale.
It can say nothing of the woman
seated in a kitchen, her fingers
teasing strands of coloured thread apart.

You cannot read the stitchery like Braille
to know the urgent young woman
with her dark hair, quick laugh, quick temper,
with her death growing
          dark and fetal in her womb.

My mother smoothes the cloth. She touches
lightly — her fingers crumpled now,
but slender as her sister's hands
who set these stitches thirty years ago.

The complex thread of grief still works
through her voice, the patterns of halt
and absence —

> *When I heard*
> *when I got the   letter   saying*
> *she would*
>   *die*

I just got into bed
and   huddled under the covers.
I wanted everything to stop
I wanted everything to go
                    black

How we still love

I.

Sometimes the overwhelming need
to tidy, to arrange, to make
insensible things comfortable.

Like the cupboard, higgeldy-piggeldy
with dolls and stuffed animals.
I would take them all out, make
the shelf soft with folded blankets.
Then tuck my toys in.

The baby doll cuddled on panda's lap.
The bride, her shiny rayon gown
and gilt curls smoothed gently, ribbons
re-tied. The little rose-cheeked dolls.
All seated in cozy circles, heels splayed,
laps covered with a friendly quilt.

And then I would tell them softly,
Don't be afraid of the dark,
though I knew they weren't,
and close the door.

2.

I cannot bear to think of you
so still and silent in a distant city. I need
to know you are tucked safely into the dark,
into the shrouding earth.

So small, you are now.
So small. The body that was
once a bride, your smile an open rose
in honeymoon photos. The body
that once curled around babies.

I cannot go about today's cold tasks
here, thinking of you there, where strangers
smooth your gray hair, your dress.

How we still love the insensible,
need to whisper   Do not be afraid.
We will not stop loving
even after we have closed
the door to go about our lives
in the bare light.

Learning to hate the tongue

Pale skin powdery, as if from the dust
of clapped erasers. Twin set and pearls,
cardigan clipped in place across her chest
by poodle brooches, puffs of real fur. Her hand,
in a white, cotton, wrist-length glove, writes
on the board, *Du bist shön wie eine Rose.*

Du — the intimate voice, explains Miss Plesch
to her high school class. A small group. German
unpopular in postwar Scarborough.
Her lips pout over the umlaut. She scolds
when I file a ragged nail in class. *So rude, rude.*
Not what a lady does in public.

A language invested with fairy-tale,
Märchen. Black Fraktur type marches jagged
through our textbooks, like the witch's peaked roof.
Something from another century.

***

Dust floating in the wheezy lecture hall.
University College, squeaking hardwood floors.
Someplace from another century. The boy beside me
wears a round cap on the crown of his head. A Jew.

We argue about the Holocaust. *You must*
put it behind you, I tell him, sure
in my young Canadian magnanimity.

***

Now you, my newest, dearest teacher.
Who can claim five thousand years of history

for your people. But whose family tale
vanished into the maw of this century.
Lodz ghetto. Warsaw. Galicia.

Millions of names fallen, leaves from a felled tree.
Your family name so common among them,
that single human beings are untraceable.

***

What we do in public:
Half a century ago, boys on the streets of Montreal,
hissed at your mother, maudite juive. The teacher
inspected her embroidered petticoat. *Such a clean
little Jewish girl* she said, surprised.

Last week, the man in my committee meeting
rubbed thumb and forefinger together —
the old Shylockian gesture — at the mention of Jews.

As if no time had elapsed.

***

Now, I hear the ach and sht of German words
behind me in a queue, and my hackles rise
slightly, like a dog at the smell of something foreign,
hostile. Prejudice has become a dark bone.
I do not like this possession, but cannot bury it.

I have learned to hate the tongue
and what it says. Words from the black root.

Juden 'raus.
Endlösung

Dirty Jew. Chink. Jap. Paki. Wog.

Goy.

The words of alienation. Words that should stick
in throats, but stain as fluently as ink spilled
on a scarred desk.

***

A century of pogrom and civil war. The litany
of extermination:
> *Hiroshima. Ukraine. Cambodia. Serbia. Angola.*

What hope from holocausts, unless perhaps
they rip open the world's shell to show
the tangled meat within — humanity's common
nerves and gut

and the shared sinews of the tongue.
Years beyond my German class, I recognize
the Yiddish words murmured
in your mother's dying ear.
Sei gesund, mother. Sei gesund.

Be well. Be well. What we must learn
from holocausts: to put them beside us,
not behind. To recognize their intimate voice

as the century swings on its millennial hinge,
the door from a savage classroom.

Lines on Culloden Battlefield

"Rubbish!"
      My aunt wears her nearly-eighty years
vehemently, like a tartan scarf flung
across her shoulders. She shakes her white-floss hair
at the tea shop, the interpretive displays, the gift
nook with its books about Lock Ness and trays
of thistle lapel pins.

We file across Culloden battlefield, wind fixed
at our chests like an English bayonet. Beyond the moor,
the broad shield of the Moray firth. Snapping flags
demark the ancient fighting lines. Boulders break
from heather — the Keppoch Stone, Clan Donald's stone.
These are the bones from which a battle
can be reconstructed. A skeleton from which the flesh
is picked as clean as ravens' leavings, after
two hundred years have gone.

We pace the graves of the clans.
Low granite fists, a drumroll of names.
Our names. MacDonald. Matheson. We contemplate
bravery and boys and stupid men and lost causes.

Then go inside the tourist centre once again.
I am grateful for the warmth and tea and scones,
however incongruous. But Aunt Kath still says,
"Rubbish."
      She doesn't want her history
dug up and tagged, explained. She learned too well
the lines drawn on this same battlefield, says
even to this day, "You can never trust a Campbell."

Place/name

They called this mountain *Buachaille
Etive Mor*: the Shepherd of Etive
Moor. It looms above the road,
closing its flock in steep-sided
pens — Glen Etive, Glen Coe —
safe from the shapeless winds
of Rannoch Moor.

Once every hill was named
in this language of loch and moorland,
its gutturals soft as the choric purr
of immense and gentle cats. Every
outcrop, every purling stream
tamed with words.

Few remember now. In the fading
of the soft language, the hills
and rocks of Etive have taken back
their names. They crouch — great, feral
beasts, subject no more
to the tongue's tending.

Landscapes

East of Lethbridge

The land lies prostrate under a patriarchal sky
that is cloudless, clean-jawed
                        handsome as a magazine.

The earth, kept in blonde bondage
              by long strips of highway, stares
up without expression.

The wind sucks her dry, complaining
        at the lack of nourishment
and grain bins stand to conical attention
like small metal nipples on desiccated breasts.

Near Hanna

Land lies in a domestic dream
a quilted landscape in the pale spring sun

its spreading pattern pieced together from fields
in textile textures prepared for sowing,

ribbed like corduroy or brown grosgrain ribbon,
flocked with distant stands of brush.

The sunlight lies down
             pillowed on a leftover hay bale.

The wide fields dip gently
like the rise and fall of blankets
            as a sleeper breaths.

Near Red Deer This land is vain and knows she is courted
                             for her wealth.
                 She lets grain trickle between the long fingers
                 left by labouring swathers
                 and lets rivers run slowly down her thighs.

                 She fingers cloth-of-gold and the embroidery
                 of wheat fields
                 colours her lips with saskatoon berries,
                 smiles seduction upwards at the sky.

South of Stettler the land collects water in small round cradles.

                 The geometry of lines grooved by swathers
                 becomes complex, curved, non-Euclidean —
                 concave reverses into convex.

                 Round hay bales nestle side by side against a rise
                 like a row of piglets crowded against teats.

                 Other hills suckle poplar stands or pines
                 that stand up to the sky.

Towards Jasper the mountains pull down clouds
                 and toss the water away impatiently.

                 They hold up scissors and cut the sky in pieces.

The winter-adapted eye

This country would be colourless
to travellers in the silver arms of planes
who cross its white and stationary acres.

I'm not at twenty thousand feet.
Though this Red Arrow bus has plush
seats and pull-down table trays, and even
an in-flight movie. Overhead, the video screens
are small vivid squares where Robin Hood
releases silent, fiery arrows. I didn't pay
$2.50 for the headset.
> I am flying home to you, wheels
> never off the ground. Vibration
> comfortable and real along my spine.

Outside, the sweet and sombre colours
of November. Snowfields wear tan stubble
like our hero's three-day growth of beard.
Gray poplar bluffs scud like low clouds. Sky
wears the douce demeanour of approaching snow.
> Robin kisses Marian. All the arrows
> shot. Leaves garland the wedding scene.
> The End.

The brilliant screen goes blank. I look outside,
adapt my eye again to winter, find the colour.
Faint maroon refrain of dogwood branches
in the ditches. Far across a field, mute ochre
hay-bales cluster like cattle seeking company.
We cross the Red Deer River, lodestone-gray.
Ice frazzils on its surface. Below, an ordinary
mystery — the water, flowing on all winter.
> Where does it come from,
> this constant current
> this happy unending?

III. Distances interlock

Space is not a lot of points close together;
it is a lot of distances interlocked
- Arthur Stanley Eddington

Eddington meant space is not a smooth, uniform set of point that make up a passive stage on which events occur. Space is actually a series of distances, relationships — from the scale over which subatomic interactions take place to the scale on which galaxies move.

1.

Place trips you up.
Sticks out its foot as you go by
on the journey through time
and brings you down

here. How did I get
here?

Bank of a northern river. I scratch
letters of my name on clay soil.
Dust scent, sun-rusted leaves
veined in red. Aster. Thistle silk
webs my throat. Brown river bends
away from me, around the
corner of my life — an artery
that links the pulse of water
to the sea.

My sister writes to me of
blue ocean by her door.
Beat and swell of water, curve
of white beach, lacing of foam,
taking her children to swim.
She and I grew up beside
a lake that curved
beyond our sight.

Jet trail overhead blurs into lace
against blue sky. Seamless sky.
Ripples of air lap past me. I have made
an accidental journey inland —
have come, of all places, here.

2.

Isobars. Isotherms. Isohels.
Geographers elaborate these lines
that loop and whorl like fingerprints
on the map's surface. Lines that connect
equalities of pressure, temperature,
hours of sunshine — the commonalties
of air. Isanthesic lines, drawn through
the places of the globe where certain plants
bloom simultaneously — a linking of lilacs.

No such ligatures connect us
now. Our temperatures turned upside
down. Your winter — my summer. My
long twilights. Your abrupt
tropic darkness that falls in gardens
where the lilac will not grow.
Your blossoms are lemon, jacaranda,
orchids like moth moons.

Instead, the lines divide us. Equator,
where the world changes direction,
where currents and seasons coil
widdershins. Date line, dividing our
todays, so that you are always in my
tomorrow, sleep while I waken, read
morning papers while I close up
the day's eye.

3.

My father hugged me as tight as the buttons
newly stitched to his raincoat. Then picked up
his suitcase, heavy in the train's dragging steam.
I hardly waved good-bye to him — too young to know
how the long months would wave farewell to me
before he waved hello.

"That's my Daddy. He's gone to Canada," I told
a small, curious spectator. Canada no further
than the train ride up to Glasgow.

Two decades later, I helped my mother pack
an overnight case with the trivial
necessities. Toothbrush. Spare pyjamas. "At least
it was a mild attack. He'll soon be home," I told
her, and rode quite calmly in the taxi across town.

Until, standing at the low gate of the hospital bed,
I saw him suddenly small, and frail — as though
he had receded into a distance. As though he lay
on a train car pulling slowly out. I began to know
how long a journey is.

4.

Your hands journey on my spine,
on the hollow of my hip. I hold you
close, I will admit
no distance between us.

I crave the blurring of distances,
of identities. As though you and I could be
waves that interlock and spread
around the pilings of a dock endlessly
in touch. Our three dimensions making one
seamless continuity.

But always, there
intercedes the Planck distance
the necessary space,
the underlying
graininess of matter. My palm
connects with the soft
blur of hair
on your shoulder.
I can get
no closer.

5.

"Mountains. Look at mountains, Rachel."

Distant peaks run like a brainwave
written in rock against the sky, jagged
as the line from an oscilloscope.
　　　We are mapping the world
for my brother's daughter — a tiny,
intense ship straining against
the hawsers his arms cord for her.

See, Rachel. Think.

Instead, she studies a stray pebble captured
tight in the chubby compass rose
of her baby fist. Pink granite veined
with quartz. Fact-sharp edges.
She must learn this distance first.

6.

This is what I imagined —
I would visit you, bring a Canadian stone —
a granddaughter's gift to your grave. I would sit
on the hill my father described, looking out
over Loch Lomond valley. Your final address.

I would feel how close we were. A few inches
of earth over your bones, stretch of skin over mine —
my wrists slight, like yours. I would feel
how time is the only distance real enough
to keep us separate.

This is what happened —
Of course I couldn't find you in the crowded,
vacant suburbs of the dead. Each plot with its own
iron-pegged lawn and boundaries. Rain
blotting out the valley.

How would you be there, fairy woman?
You to whom no property would stick.
Who gave away even memories, kept only
poems at the end. You recited them like charms
against death and the nurses.

Where could I find you again, ever?
Except, perhaps, under the hill
where the good folk keep their hall, avoid iron.
Where unsuspecting wanderers arrive and find
seven years gone in a night. Where time
annihilates itself, creates
space.

7.

Humankind has measured distance
with many units — pipefuls, prayers, tales
and songs. In Bengal, so they say, wayfarers
pick branches and mark their wilting.
One wilted branch — one ka.

We are stretched, a thin web
of blood, a tissue of relation,
over the globe's three quarters.
I can hear your voices
on the telephone or
on tape recorders, telling poems
and stories.

But how many songs would it take
until I reached you all, tied you
together in my arms? How many
branches would wither
and leaf again, while I set one foot
in front of the other, in search
of you — only to find myself stranded
at land's end, where the ocean
curved away from me, barrier
and bond.

A leaf, dry and ridged along the veins
like an elderly hand, revolves
on brown water at my feet. It drifts
towards the bend where
the river's course deflects
with accidents of landscape
and history. I set a twig afloat
to follow it, measure in my mind
a distance to the sea.

1V. Summing over two

Lapidary

I will wear amethyst —
        an amulet to cool love ardours,
        a stone for sobriety,

        and in this way stave off
        the pounding heart and trembling
        of my hands, the bitter aftermath
        of love you left behind
        after you broke the glass
        spilled purple wine.

I will wear agate
        against wakefulness, against
        the black holes of the night
        through which you disappeared,
        left my bed empty.

        I will myself become black-banded
        stone, pulled in around myself,
        impervious to memory
        or dreams.

I will wear jacinth
        the amulet for travellers,
        to assure me hospitality
        in the hearts of strangers.

        I will look for night's lodging
        and a resting place.

I will wear blue stones
        — sapphire and lapis lazuli —
        for clear seeing, for casting out

impurities of the eye
and I will look carefully
on new lovers.

I will wear ruby
          red stones staunch the flow
          of blood from wounds, and rubies
          worn on the left side
          are for living in love.

          The stone will guard my fruit trees
          and my vineyards from injury
          by tempests and fill the cup again
          with concord.

Brideprice

Next time, I shall demand
down payment, dowry, rings.
I'll ask for emerald.

Emeralds are worn by happy wives
and break when worn
by faithless husbands.
        Good value for the money —
        a stone that's decorative
        and practical withall.

Emeralds reveal the truth,
sharpen the wits and cure
diseases of the eye.
        He'll hoodwink me no longer
        with fairy stories —
        business trips, forsooth.

Emeralds placed underneath the tongue
endow a speaker with prophetic gifts.
        He'll catch the sharp edge
        of my scold's tongue, if I catch
        the same old future in his eye.

Emeralds are placed on the left hand
of those who die too young. He'd better watch
        where his hands go,
        or he will find himself
        coffined untimely.

We were failed alchemists

like so many who hope to turn years into silver
and golden anniversaries. We made only paper —
documents that cut our tongues with thin wounds —
and ordinary tin.

It may have been the fault of our equipment —
the crucible in which experiments occurred:
A small house, in suburbs so new, I half expected
to see ghost cows graze on pasture
that lay beneath the bedroom rug.

We were haunted by the ghost of promised
union — the merging touch of the alchemist's
stone, the concealed identity of kind that
must exist behind our different natures.
But love turned stone and we stayed
separate — stubborn, stoppered flasks.

It was the old, noble, greedy wish for gold
and immortality in another's eyes. It ended, like
so many experiments, in sullen lead.
I did learn something of the art of holding heat
at constant temperatures, something of the need
for pure ingredients.

A ghost approaches: the year that would have been
our silver anniversary. I find that I have,
after all, achieved amalgam. Time has distilled
its nine-times-filtered residue, evaporated
at the bottom of the cup — a dust of pain
and kindness.

aubade

You are reckless to leave my bed this way.

The ancients would smooth the sheets on rising
to be sure the imprint of their bodies, the hollows
of the night, could not be used against them.

Are you not afraid of leaving me this power,
this hold on you? Are you not afraid
that I will take this single hair, this dark line
on my pillow, and write it into spells that bind you?

But no. You leave the pattern of your body
blithely; you do not need to stay. I try
to bind you with the tangible — the key
to my front door, a toothbrush in the holder

but cannot hold you. I say the reckless words
of love. You kiss me farewell and leave
the rumpled sheets, your imprint here on me.

Loss of faith

I wish I came as trusting as a novice comes
to her devotions, certain in their promises.
I wish that in the quiet times, the hours
of silent thought, I did not hear
the failing words of past fidelities.

> Trust in me and I
> shall not desert you.

That others told me lies — this should not
undermine my faith in truth. That I had houses
built on sand — this should not shift my faith
in rock. But sand is only rock worn down
by time. Time converts much, and you cannot know
how much I fear apostasy.

The foreign wife

Your god would be my god.

I came to you from a foreign country, still
young, gleaning love from the dry furrows.
Still supple as willow, still willing to put
my hand on a stranger's door. You were
grave and kindly, your words a refuge.

> *But you keep me in a place*
> *apart, a wall between me*
> *and the murmur of voices*
> *in the temple. A veil*
> *conceals me.*
> *You do me the courtesy*
> *of exclusion. Concubine,*
> *not wife.*

Growing here against a sunseared wall,
far from my people, my arms
stretch out. They ache to give you
everything, to return the dower of grain
and goodness.

> *I am a pear ripening*
> *on a window sill, severed*
> *from the branch that bore it.*
> *Still capable of achieving*
> *sweetness.*

Your kindness is sweeter than
oranges. But my arms are pained
from holding out unwanted fruit, droop
with the fear of a harsh harvest, the fear
your nomad tribe will fold its tents,

will drive its flocks away to some other
country, rumoured to be warm
with god's breath.

> I am jealous of your god, who is
> jealous as any wife. The god of walls
> and veils.

I see it in your eyes, the hope
your god will find delight in you,
will lead you to the place he calls
the married land. When will I waken
in an empty courtyard? A spaliered tree
staked in place, its trunk thickening
and twisted, its roots plucking
dry soil.

Safekeeping

you have come into my keeping
you are rare and treasurable, you are
a breastplate

> the inlaid weight of gems and hard
> worked metal

> you lie pressed against me
> bone to white ivory, sardonyx and chalcedony
> on my breasts

> inscribing in my flesh the letters
> of the ancient language.

you have come into my keeping
you are rare and wield power, you are
a talisman

> hidden in a staff, a chrysoprase
> concealed to concentrate its strength

> a jewel with the virtue of shining
> in the dark, you are gold-green light
> the oldest luminance, you are

> thrust for safekeeping
> into my guarded heart

Filial son

> *The filial son will move as though he carried*
> *a jade symbol or a full vessel. Still*
> *and grave, absorbed in what he is doing,*
> *he will seem as though he were unable*
> *to sustain the burden and in danger*
> *of letting it fall.*
> — *Confucius*

You bear your father's memory like a full bowl
of tears, balanced precisely so that none will spill
although they tremble at the rim. A loss so old
it lies in your pocket like a jade pebble
worn smooth by the wilful stream.

    You were then so young, so
young. Your face thin as a brush
tip. Your hair black — a horizontal sweep
of ink. Now your face has patiently
assumed the character of his,
a tribute paid without your will
or knowledge.

    Sometimes now you see
his picture, so familiar on your desk,
as though you looked with a stranger's eyes
and fear this is a lapse, a lessening.
In sleep, your tongue calls out his name
— a ritual, half talisman,
half plea you will not fail in honour,
in fidelity.

Apprentice

I have learned this trade of loving
through the years, indentured then
to others. I learned my letters well,
the patient craft improving
and wrote a fair and flowing hand
for other lovers
                    with such tools
as they gave me —
vellum more or less unmarred
and nibs that scratched more
or less smoothly on the parchment.

I had my moments,
                    patches of illumination
while copying the paragraphs —
contractual undertakings, writs
and assignations.

I did not realize I was apprenticed
to this trade of hearts, to this exchange
of hands. You give me gold leaf
to work with and flowering lines.
You give me words I never thought
to write.

klein bottle

love is all surface
klein bottle   plane
surface without
end   wrapped
round   curve
of shoulder   around thigh
surface penetrating
surface   world
made two-manifold
too   manifold world
without end   surface without
seam   and it seems
I could go
nowhere else.

Note: A Klein bottle is the three-dimensional equivalent of a Mobius strip; wherever you start on its surface, you can reach any point on that surface, whether inside or out. In other words, it has only one side. Mathematically, it is classified as a "two-manifold," along with other surfaces like the torus.

Algorithmic compressibility

Any string of symbols that can be given an abbreviated representation is called "algorithmically compressed."
- John Barrow

Algorithm: that simple sum
thing under pressure, waiting
to fizz up.

Saturday luxuriance. The lazy algebra of blankets,
brackets curled around digits, in addition to
the blank non-light of morning in December.

"Take zero, add two; take
the sum, add two." That simple
string of symbols, and you create
all the even integers — half
the numbers of the universe.

Burrowing nose in blankets, I arrive at the scent
of making love. The compression chamber lid pops off.
I want the rhythms of your body, the summing over two.

"Algorithm," from the Arabic
Al-Kwarisme. Symbols written
in sensual, satin-quilted strokes.
Thousand and one nights.

But you are already subtract, gone off about your
morning calculations. Your side is cool
negative space. And I meant to get up early, clean
the house. (It's clearly time to change
the sheets.) I close my eyes, press both duty
and desire beneath my pillow, compact words.

Seal in the bay

Sun on the inlet. Tethered
creak of the dock riding
heavy timbered posts. Wood
grain presses against my feet.

When a seal lifts its round head
barely a yard away. A pup,
quizzical and whiskered. He regards me
solemnly, paddling to stay in place

and for some reason, I think
of how you'd like a dog
but are willing to make do
with just the cat and me.

The seal pup slips back below.
I see its sturdy body bend
into its element, against the water's
long stroke. I will carry you

this tale, something round and warm
to give you, to tell you how I move
in your regard — my essential element,
the grain against my skin, the sun let in.

V. Epithalamion

A reminder - *the epithalamion or wedding poem flourished in the sixteenth and seventeenth centuries. Typically, these were long poems following the events of the marriage day — the bridegroom rising eagerly, the dressing of the bride (always, of course, virginal), the invitation and arrival of the guests, the ceremony, the feast, and the retirement to the nuptial bed. Poets frequently called on classical figures of Greek and Roman mythology to bless the union.*

The form reached a high point in Edmund Spenser's Epithalamion, written to celebrate his own marriage in 1597. Each of his metrically intricate stanzas ends with a chorus — a variation on "The woods to me shall answer and the echoes ring."

The sequence of poems in the following pages build on this traditional form and turn it around. It is how a woman of the twentieth century would write a poem to celebrate her marriage — a middle-aged woman, not virginal, marrying across the old and new worlds.

"Huppah" is the canopy held over the couple during a Jewish wedding ceremony; "gladdening the bride" is an ancient Jewish tradition of singing her praises.

Epithalamion

The bride wakens

gropes for her glasses on the nightstand.
In the darkness that will taper soon
into dawn, I swing my feet clear of this
convent-narrow bed. Look up to see
the Dipper — a silver-handled cup
filling up the dark breadth of window
completely, like a wedding picture
in a frame, the happy beginning.

Seven brilliant stars with ancient names —
Alkaid, Mizar, Alioth...
   Their bright bodies shape
a pattern old as the human mind, connected
by the brain's compulsive threads.

The Wagon. The Bear. The Drinking Gourd.
Its bowl turned up to catch the pulse
of starlight spilled over fields.

   In that cup's distilled light,
   earth's faint scent on its dark, cool lip,
   I pledge you.

These night-fallow fields echo
coyote yip, muskrat rustle. Here grow
sweetgrass and poplar.

Not oak groves and twining eglantine.
No dryads to bear the bridal train,
No Hymen with his flaming torch and coronal.

I left them on the far side of oceans crossed
long ago, and await my wedding day
in a new world — a world neither pagan
nor classical, a world impossibly old
with other gods.

The day's arrival

Horizon is still a faint seam stitched
against the wine-dark earth.

Come quickly, day.
Summer has already turned past the solstice.
I want no more delay. If only
if
        if only I could have come to you
more quickly. Could have cut
short the string of fumbling years
when we were in the same world,
and didn't even know it.

Yet moved always closer, our lives
pulled into proximity at last.
Gravity must have been the path of least
resistance, the shape of space between us,
so the long ellipse of my life turned out to be
the straightest, simplest way to you.

Gravity was the slope down which my pinball heart
had to run, regardless of the bells and flippers
placed in its way.

> From this stone cup,
> heavy in the hand, cut from the bone

of the planet that travels
so constantly around the sun,
I pledge you.

The horizon thread unwinds at last, expands.
Now comes dawn with her cupped hands.
Light laces roadsides and the ditches filled
with mirrors and bouquets. A procession
of asters — earth stars — queen anne's lace
and sceptered goldenrod. Garnet-berried
kinnick-kinnick strewn at our feet.

Summer, full-hipped and farthingaled,
has come to court.

The guests arrive

Your guests arrive
        ghosts
grieving eyes that watch
from the shadows of your history.

Those who are lost
under gravestones.
Those who are lost
from the towns and shtetl.

Those who would believe you lost to them,
a runnel of precious water sinking
into dry foreign sands.

Those for whom you light memory candles
your head bowed, tears recollecting,
as you travel to a country of the past
where I can never follow.

The voices of Jews, the faces of Jews
pouring through streets to synagogue.
The high holy days, the shofar calling
through rain falling straight and fine and silver
as the fringes of a prayer shawl.

> *From the empty cup of exile,*
> *engraved with the pattern of a star,*
> *the grief-edged sign of Solomon*
> *I pledge you.*

The wedding gift

This I cannot give you.
>   What God so lightly promised Abraham —
>   descendants numberless as stars
>   that seed the night sky.

This I cannot give you.
>   A son to say for you, a boy who will remember
>   in your death, your life and tell again
>   the tale of your existence.

This I cannot give you.
>   I, who would give you all the stars. I am barren
>   as old Sarah, sending her servant's body
>   to her husband's bed.

This only can I give you.
>   These handmaiden words, clumsy ministers
>   to gladden you and praise the kindness
>   of your hands, the sweetness of your mouth.

From the glass that will be shattered,
fragile as a human life, fragrant as the wine it holds,
I pledge you my truth.

The exchange of promises

I will cut my wedding gown
from maps of far places,
lay the pattern of my life
on the cloth of new cities,
join you where the roads cross.

I will rise and fasten
columbine and yarrow in my hair,
join you where the sun
stands stitched to the axis
of the far-spinning year.

I will cut the clinging threads
of old mornings, cleave to you
from this day forward. Our bodies
will cross like the twin blades
of scissors, love at the hinge
of our days.

The marriage bed

Soft-palmed night returns and spreads
its huppah over us, embroidery of stars —
the patterns of our past and future
the shapes we make of sky.

The guests have left us with their wishes,
here in this tabernacle, this curtained space
twined from our lives,
pliable and green as poplar boughs.

The fields are silent once again, and the planet
travels further on its path. Our bodies
softly come together, pulled by gravity.
My hand cradling your cheek,
our mouths filled.

> *I am yours in body and in spirit*
> *now and ever. From the shining*
> *cup of worlds,   old and always new,*
> *thereto I plight thee*
> *my troth.*

The open hand

The monkey likeness of it.
The quilting of its surface. The fingers
curved to form a shallow bowl.
The crescent nails that rise along
the curved horizon of fingertips.
The thumb a tree limb branching off
but growing, ultimately
in the same direction. The whole
contrivance made for grasping,
held open by an act of will.

The lines of life and heart form
tributary systems, determined
by the lift and dip of uplands,
valleys and high moors.
On this topology appears now
one thing, now another. A scrap
of lace, rough and intricate as fur.
A child's barette, wonderfully clear
in plastic. A fading tulip petal, curled
at the edges, soft as the crumpled light
of dusk.

Each surface rests a time against
skin — membrane that divides,
contains, connects. Sometimes,
fingers curve protectively
like a child desiring
to cage thistledown. But then
flex outwards once again.
The openness is all.